Australian Birds

A Celebration

Illustrations by Shirley Barber
Written and edited by Margaret Geddes

The Five Mile Press

The Five Mile Press Pty Ltd
1 Centre Road, Scoresby
Victoria 3179 Australia
www.fivemile.com.au

First published 2012

Printed in China

Design by Sardine Design

National Library of Australia cataloguing-in-publication data available on request.

ISBN: 9781742482637

'…few other creatures seem so alive in every fibre…so fully given to the action, whether in song, in motion or in display. Even in quiescence, they are concentrations of vitality.'

Saint-John Perse (1887–1975)

Contents

Eastern Yellow Robin, *Eopsaltria australis*

Introduction

Birds live alongside us in a way no other creatures do. They live independent lives yet they share our space…or perhaps we share theirs.

And they also offer us so much pleasure. A magpie taking a bath on a hot summer's day is a joy to behold; an eagle soaring through the open sky can take your breath away; a flock of cockatoos chattering as they fossick for feed will make you smile. Listen to the song of the butcher bird that floats in the air and you will find your day enriched.

Shirley Barber's birds remind us of the beauty and wonder that is free for us to enjoy.

For our part, let's do our best to ensure that our environment is one in which these birds can not only survive, but thrive. When our neglect may lead to a species' extinction, a little attention seems a small price to pay.

Margaret Geddes

Attracting Birds to Your Garden

Birds are looking for more than food in a garden: they are looking for perching sites, nesting places, shelter and water.

The particular trees and shrubs in your garden will influence the type of birds it attracts. Native plants, particularly those with red or yellow flowers, attract native birds. But beware! If you plant predominantly nectar plants, like grevilleas, the big wattle birds you attract will chase away smaller birds.

The Smoker Parrot

He has the full moon on his breast,
The moonbeams are about his wing;
He has the colours of a king.
I see him floating unto rest
When all eyes wearily go west,
And the warm winds are quieting.
The moonbeams are about his wing:
He has the full moon on his breast.

John Shaw Neilson, 1911

❖ ❖

Regent Parrot, *Polytelis anthopeplus*

An Epitome of Joyousness

Birds are as essential to a living garden as flowers and greenery. My honeyeaters are always there, winter and summer, because I have planted the shrubs which attract them; those shrubs which are most prolific nectar carriers.

I get living rainbows at leisure on these false spring days, when the hose is playing in fine spray on a shrubbery. The Eastern Spinebill, that epitome of joyousness, dives in and out, making colour flashes.

Then he sits and sings to us from a budding rondeletin bush, which will soon be a riot of colour and a penthouse of perfume.

This honeyeater is an all-the-year visitor. A procession of his kind comes along in endless stream for the stored riches we offer.

From 'A Garden of Birds', Waratah [P.J. Hurley], Sydney Morning Herald, 17 August 1946

Eastern Spinebill, *Acanthorhynchus tenuirostris*

Food for Thought

Though wild birds are best left to their own devices, feeding them is a temptation that few bird lovers can resist. If possible, cater for visiting birds on a more permanent basis by creating a garden that offers them food, shelter and nesting spaces. That way you are free to take holidays without disturbing the birds' daily diet.

If you choose to artificially feed native birds, research the species to ensure that the food you are offering is good for them. Kitchen scraps are not the ideal diet and neither are all commercial parrot seeds, many of which contain a surfeit of fattening sunflower seeds.

Offer a limited amount of food for a short time, about fifteen minutes, then remove and dispose of the leftovers, which may attract unwanted guests. Place fresh water in a clean container, either in a secure spot or an open area in which birds can see predators approach.

Rainbow Lorikeet, *Trichoglossus haematodus*

Which Plants Attract Which Birds?

The banksias offer nectar, seed and nesting sites, and like the heaths and melaleucas in flower, attract honeyeaters in particular.

Eucalypts attract rosellas and lorikeets, which feed on the blossoms and seeds.

Grevillea and bottlebrush offer nectar and shelter and in Queensland attract lorikeets and honeyeaters.

Dense spiky shrubs, such as the hakeas and some of the more prickly acacias (wattles), can provide refuge as well as nectar, seeds, pollen and nesting sites for wrens and finches.

Native grasses, such as kangaroo and wallaby grass, will also provide seeds for the finches.

The fruit of the lilly pilly provides food for lorikeets, wrens, finches, cockatoos and galahs.

The native fuchsia, which bears bell-shaped flowers between March and October, attracts nectar feeders like honeyeaters, wattlebirds and rosellas.

Purple Crowned Lorikeet, *Glossopsitta porphyrocephala*

Australia's Critically Endangered Birds

Australia has far too many birds
classified as 'critically endangered'.
These birds are on the brink of
extinction, but can be saved by
conscientious conservation.

Azure Kingfisher, *Alcedo azurea*

Common name	Scientific name
Abbott's Booby	*Papasula abbotti*
Amsterdam Albatross	*Diomedea amsterdamensis*
Azure Kingfisher (Tasmanian)	*Alcedo azurea diemenensis*
Blue Petrel	*Halobaena caerulea*
Brown Goshawk (Christmas Island)	*Accipiter fasciatus natalis*
Brown Thornbill (King Island)	*Acanthiza pusilla archibaldi*
Chatham Albatross	*Thalassarche eremita*
Christmas Island Frigatebird	*Fregata andrewsi*
Christmas Island Hawk-owl	*Ninox natalis*
Christmas Island Imperial-pigeon	*Ducula whartoni*
Christmas Island White-eye	*Zosterops natalis Coxen's*
Fig-parrot	*Cyclopsitta diophthalma coxeni*
Eastern Bristlebird (northern)	*Dasyornis brachypterus monoides*
Emerald Dove (Christmas Island)	*Chalcophaps indica natalis*
Glossy Swiftlet (Christmas Island)	*Collocalia esculenta natalis*
Helmeted Honeyeater	*Lichenostomus melanops cassidix*
Herald Petrel	*Pterodroma heraldica*
Island Thrush (Christmas Island)	*Turdus poliocephalus erythropleurus*
Night Parrot	*Pezoporus occidentalis*
Orange-bellied Parrot	*Neophema chrysogaster*
Pied Currawong (western Victoria)	*Strepera graculina ashbyi*
Round Island Petrel	*Pterodroma arminjoniana*
Scrubtit (King Island)	*Acanthornis magnus greenianus*
Soft-plumaged Petrel (northern)	*Pterodroma mollis deceptornis*
Southern Emu-wren (Fleurieu Peninsula)	*Stipiturus malachurus intermedius*
Spotted Quail-thrush (Mt Lofty Ranges)	*Cinclosoma punctatum anachoreta*
Star Finch (southern)	*Neochmia ruficauda ruficauda*
Wandering Albatross	*Diomedea exulans*
White-chested White-eye	*Zosterops albogularis*
White-tailed Tropicbird (Christmas Island)	*Phaethon lepturus fulvus*
Yellow Chatt	*Epthianura crocea macgregori*

This list is from the Action Plan for Australian Birds 2000 by Stephen Garnett and Gabriel Crowley.

Our Feathered Friends

The company of humans is enjoyed by some birds more than others.

Some, like sparrows, seagulls and pigeons, seek us out, confident that we will provide their next meal.

Others tolerate us, and happily let us share their space. One such bird is the Olive-backed Sunbird (also known as the Yellow-bellied Sunbird), which is both cheeky and bold.

This tropical bird is found in southern China, and down through southern Asia to north-eastern Australia.

The little sunbirds are monogamous and the pairs build their distinctive pendulous nests together, using bark, moss and lichen and whatever useful materials they can find. Once the eggs hatch, both male and female care for the young for the two to three weeks until they are ready to leave.

Though they feed their young insects, the adults feed mainly on nectar and many choose to nest in tropical parks and gardens, though their original habitat was the mangroves. The sunbirds are comfortable around people, and sometimes suspend their nests from balconies and verandahs.

Sociable to man extremely, building and nestling and rustling about him,—prying and speculating, curiously watchful of him at his work, if likely to be profitable to themselves, or even sometimes in mere pitying sympathy, and wonder how such a wingless, beakless creature can do anything.

John Ruskin, Love's Meinie, 1873

Olive-backed Sunbird, *Nectarinia jugularis*

Coming to the Rescue

If you find a sick, injured or orphaned bird in your yard, first lock up any pet cats or dogs that may be a threat. Then quietly observe the bird long enough to confirm that it does indeed need your help.

Pick up the bird, using a towel or soft cloth, and place in a quiet dark area, such as a cardboard box (don't forget to make airholes). It will need warmth, so you could line the box with a cloth-wrapped heating pad or hot water bottle.

Keep in mind, some birds are dangerous to handle and take care. Unless you have had previous experience, do not try to administer first aid yourself. And do not force food or water on the bird. You may do more harm than good.

Call for assistance. Try your local vet first – most vets will see an injured bird free of charge. Or call your local animal rescue centre for advice.

If you find a baby bird that has fallen from a nest that is within your reach, replace it. Birds have very little sense of smell and, contrary to common belief, will not reject their young if touched by a human hand.

Eastern Shrike-tit, *Falcunculus frontatus*

A Very Noble Bird

Dutch explorer Willem de Vlamingh was attempting to rescue survivors of a ship that had gone missing from the Dutch East Indies when he sailed into the Swan River in 1696 and saw his first black swan.

Though he charted some of the west coast of a new continent, it was his tale of the black swan that shook European certainties back home. Until then, all swans were white and 'black swan' was an expression used to describe an unlikely proposition. The poet Juvenal in 84 AD described the perfect wife as 'a rare bird in the lands, and very like a black swan'.

In Australia, black swans were in abundance, as the British discovered when they established a penal colony in Sydney almost one hundred years later.

According to the Nyungar people of the south-west of Western Australia, their ancestors were black swans who became men. The black swan is now the bird emblem of Western Australia.

On this lake, they first observed a black swan, which species, though proverbially rare in other parts of the world, is here by no means uncommon, being found on most lakes. This is a very noble bird, and equally beautiful in form. On being shot at, it rose and discovered that its wings were edged with white: the bill was tinged with red.

Arthur Phillip, The Voyage of Governor Phillip to Botany Bay, 1789

Black Swan, *Cygnus atratus*

Larrikin of the Bush

The Laughing Kookaburra suffered the ignoble title of the 'laughing jackass' among Australia's early settlers until the 1860s when its indigenous name was adopted. The name 'kookaburra', which mimics the bird's call, comes from the language of the Wiradjuri people who lived west of the Blue Mountains in central New South Wales. The kookaburra is the state of New South Wales' bird emblem.

Its peculiar gurgling laugh, commencing from a low, and gradually rising to a high and loud tone, is often heard by the traveller in all parts of the colony, sending forth its deafening noises whilst remaining perched on the lofty branch of a tree watching for prey; it is respected by gardeners for destroying grubs, &c. It is not uncommon to see these birds fly up with a long snake pending from their beak, the bird holding the reptile by the neck, just behind the head…This is the first bird heard in the morning, and the last (among the day birds) at night; it rises with the dawn, when the woods re-echo with its gurgling laugh, and at sunset they are again heard.

Bennet's Wanderings, Hobart Town Courier, 10 April 1835

Laughing Kookaburra, *Dacelo novaeguineae*

The Forest
Floor Sampler

The Superb Lyrebird is the world's third largest songbird. It lives in the forests of south-eastern Australia where the male builds a large mound about fifteen centimetres high on which to stand and sing to attract females. The male lyrebird in full display is breathtaking, not least because of the song it sings. Each sings a unique song that intermingles mimicry of the other birdsongs and sounds in the forest.

Superb Lyrebird, *Menura novaehollandiae*

26 January 1798.

The ground very rocky and brushey, so that we could scarce pass... We saw several sorts of dung of different animals, one of which Wilson called a Whom-batt, which is an animal about 20 inches high with short legs and a very thick body forwards with a large head, round ears, and very small eyes, is very fat, and has much the appearance of a badger. There is another animal which the natives call a Cullawine (a koala), which much resembles the Sloths in America. Here I shot a bird about the size of a pheasant, but the tail of it very much resembles a Peacock, with large long feathers, which are white, orange and lead colour, and black at the ends; its body betwixt a brown and green, brown under his neck and black upon his head. Black legs and very strong claws.

From the diary of John Price, servant to New South Wales' second governor John Hunter.

A Couple of Dazzlers

The Eclectus Parrot is one of those very rare birds – about two per cent of all bird species – in which the female is brighter and more flamboyant than its mate. For some time the male, with his predominantly green feathers and orange beak, and the red-blue female were thought to belong to different species.

In the wild, the Eclectus Parrot is found in far north Australia, on the tip of the Cape York Peninsular, and in New Guinea. They live high up in the rainforests and nest deep in the hollows of trees more than twenty-five metres off the ground.

The nesting females spend many months a year guarding their nest hollow. The males will fly for up to ten kilometres above the trees in search of fruit, seeds, nuts and nectar, which they regurgitate on their return to feed the female and any young.

The male in flight would be vulnerable to hawks and birds of prey flying above them, but for their green colouring, which allows them to blend in with the rainforest canopy.

The Eclectus Parrot's highly intelligent and inquisitive nature makes them suitable pets. They are fine talkers and rival the African Grey Parrot in their ability to learn a large vocabulary. They also love to sing.

Eclectus Parrot, *Eclectus roratus*

The Turquoise Parrot

The Turquoise Parrot was almost extinct in the wild one hundred years ago, but the population recovered, and is now found in south-east Queensland, New South Wales and north-east Victoria. It remains vulnerable in New South Wales and threatened in Victoria, due in part to the widespread clearance of its preferred grassy woodland habitat.

Mother Parrot's Advice to her Children

Never get up till the sun gets up,
Or the mists will give you a cold,
And a parrot whose lungs have once been touched
Will never live to be old.
Never eat plums that are not quite ripe,
For perhaps they will give you a pain:
And never dispute what the hornbill says,
Or you'll never dispute again.
Never despise the power of speech:
Learn every word as it comes,
For this is the pride of the parrot race,
That it speaks in a thousand tongues.
Never stay up when the sun goes down,
But sleep in your own home bed,
And if you've been good, as a parrot should,
You will dream that your tail is red.

From Uganda, Africa, translated by A.K. Nyabongo

Turquoise Parrot, *Neophema pulchella*

First Impressions

SOME ACCOUNT OF THAT PART OF NEW HOLLAND NOW CALLED NEW SOUTH WALES

Birds there were Several Species of – sea fowl, Gulls, Shaggs, Soland geese or Gannets of 2 sorts, Bobies, etc. and Pelicans of an enormous size, but these last tho we saw many thousands of them were so shy that we never got one of them; as were the Cranes also of which we saw several very Large and some beautifull species. In the Rivers were ducks who flew in large flocks but were very hard to come at, and on the Beach were curlews of several sorts, some very like our English ones, and Many small Beach Birds. The Land Birds were crows, very like if not quite the same as our English ones, Parrots and Paraquets most Beautifull, White and black Cocatoes, Pidgeons, beautifull Doves, Bustards, and many others which did not at all resemble those of Europe. Most of these were extremely shy, so that it was with difficulty that we shot any of them…

From *The Endeavour Journal of Sir Joseph Banks*, August 1770

Australian King Parrot, *Alisterus scapularis*

Lofty as a King

The Great Egret, also known in Australia as a white crane, is found throughout the world. It is one of Australia's colonial waterbirds, a sociable group of species that includes the ibises, egrets, herons and spoonbills. These wading birds breed in colonies, often in close proximity to other species.

This regal bird's long slender neck is almost one and a half times its body height and its yellow bill is sharp and effective in spearing fish, frogs and insects in shallow water. A demand for the beautiful plume feathers it develops during the breeding season almost led to its extinction last century.

Its habitat is freshwater wetlands, river shallows, tidal mudflats and irrigation areas, and its life has been made more difficult by our diminished river systems and recent drought. In Victoria the Great Egret is an endangered bird.

There was a lake I loved in gentle rain:
One day there fell a bird, a courtly crane:
Wisely he walked, as one who knows of pain.

Gracious he was and lofty as a king:
Silent he was, and yet he seemed to sing
Always of little children and the Spring.

From 'The Gentle Water Bird', John Shaw Neilson, 1924

Great Egret, *Ardea alba*

Talking Back

Australia abounds in talking birds: parrots, cockatoos, parakeets and cockatiels, and one of the world's best talkers is native to Australia: the budgerigar.

Talking birds mimic human speech and some pet budgies have learned hundreds of words and phrases. Compared with many parrots, they are also comparatively docile. They chatter, whistle and cheep, and they enjoy human attention.

Budgerigars in the wild are nomadic and are found in Australia's arid and semi-arid areas. The birds survive in this dry country by following thunderstorms and they forage for seed among the grasses around waterholes.

They came!

Through long unmeasured years of spaciousness
This land was joyous in the sound of wings,
Of chirp and trill, whistle and rolling note,
When flocked the quarrion and gay galah,
And on his tree the lordly cockatoo
His sentinel set. The very grasses moved
As though alive where shawls of grass-teeks crept,
Or where the waves of budgerigah flowed out,
That still in our untrammelled North sweep on
In flights leagues wide, that like a land-surf rise and fall.

From 'The Birds', Mary Gilmore, 1939

Budgerigar, *Melopsittacus undulatus*

The Passing of Parrot Pies

The abundance of colourful native parrots was a source of delight to Australia's early white settlers. Parrots were familiar in the old world and offered comfort in a land where so much of the natural world – such as the kangaroo and the platypus – was strange and new.

With around fifty-five species, including grass parrots, rosellas, lorikeets, galahs, parakeets and cockatoos, the parrots were a conspicuous part of the colony's bird life. Many were shot and turned into parrot pies or roasted, with parrots, rosellas and cockatoos used to supplement familiar game birds, such as ducks and pigeons. Various Aboriginal tribes also caught and roasted parrots.

In one sense, parrots talked their way out of the cooking pot. By the mid-19th century, their value as pets had made it more profitable for hunters to capture and transport them to England as live specimens for zoos or collectors. They were also pretty tough eating and, by the 1940s, parrot pie was no longer on the menu.

The Wit and the Parrot

Quoth a wit, 'Pretty Parrot you chatter by rote,
And the full patient dotard that taught you
'His penny took pains to convert to a groat,
And fleec'd the mere nincom that bought you.'

'In all things we differ,' the parrot return'd,
'Except in our talent for preaching,
'We parrots converse not until we are learn'd,
'You wits prate for want of good teaching.'

Sydney Gazette, 8 January 1804

Crimson Rosella, *Platycercus elegans*

The Emu and its Chicks

The emu and the red kangaroo support Australia's coat of arms, and are the best-known symbols of our native fauna. And the emu observed at Avoca Creek in 1862 was most likely male rather than female. We know now that it is the male emu that both incubates the eggs and looks after the chicks for up to eighteen months.

'Old Bushman' [Horace Wheelwright] writes: In the whole of the animal kingdom there are few more interesting birds than the emu. In a domesticated or tame state it is extremely playful and excessively mischievous…

Some years ago, a Mr. Ellis had a station on the Avoca Creek, called Avoca Forest. As often happened when emus were more numerous…a young emu had been caught and tamed. When it grew up to maturity it went away from the station, and was not seen or heard of for many weeks. One day there was a high flood in the river, and the long-lost pet made its appearance on the side of the river opposite to the homestead…The favourite was not alone, but accompanied by ten or twelve young chicks.

Every one about the homestead came out to see the mother and her brood, all wondering how she could be got over the swollen river or creek. She soon settled the question by plunging in and swimming over, leaving the young ones behind. Having landed on the western bank she then recrossed, when a young one jumped upon her back and was safely punted over. Crossing and recrossing, taking only one at a time, she thus carried the whole brood safely over, and walked them up to the station were they all remained, and were brought up in a state of perfect tameness…

Emus take to the water readily, and are capital swimmers, but I had never before, nor have I since, heard of such a display of instinct almost amounting to reason, as that of first crossing, as it were, to see if the landing was good, or the navigation practicable, and then returning to carry over the helpless offspring.

Sydney Morning Herald, 7 March 1862

Emu *(Dramaius novahollandiae)* and chicks.

I Hereby Promise...

The Gould League of Bird Lovers has been educating Australia's children about our native birds for more than one hundred years.

The league was started in 1909, under the guiding hand of Prime Minister Alfred Deakin. Its supporters were concerned about the future of some Australian species, as bird traders, egg collectors and hunters decimated their numbers in the wild.

Many will be familiar with the Gould League of Bird Lovers from primary school days, when children would pledge their support for the league and its objectives.

Its methods have varied over the years, from colouring books and posters to wildlife cam and websites, but the league still exists and its aim remain the same: to offer educational leadership in the preservation of Australia's bird life.

The Bird Lovers Pledge 1909

1. I hereby promise that I will protect native birds and will not collect their eggs.

2. I also promise that I will endeavour to prevent others from injuring native birds and destroying their eggs.

The Gould League was named in honour of Australia's earliest ornithologist, John Gould. With his wife Elizabeth, a talented nature artist, Gould visited Australia in 1838 and travelled throughout the continent to collect and classify native birds. On his return to England, he published The Birds of Australia, which on completion included eight volumes and 681 illustrations.

THE GOULD LEAGUE OF BIRD LOVERS
OF NEW SOUTH WALES

1910   1936

Membership Card

THIS IS TO CERTIFY THAT

Saltbush Canaries

The Orange and Crimson Chats were called saltbush canaries by early Australian bushmen. The Orange Chat is a beautiful dainty bird and the male in full breeding colours is a deep golden orange with a black throat. Its call is similar to the call of the canary, though more muted.

Australian chats are honeyeaters, and the Orange Chat is found in the arid interior of the continent. They live among the samphire bushes, which grow on the edge of salt lakes and claypans. They also eat both winged and ground insects and spend a lot of time on the ground, running, rather than hopping, through the scrub.

The Orange Chats build their cup-shaped nests close to the ground in the saltbush and both male and female incubate the eggs and feed the young. They go to great lengths to protect their young from their predators, the crows and the butcherbirds. They dart back and forth through the scrub in an apparent restless fervour, and manage to deliver insects to their young without revealing the site of the nest.

Orange Chat, *Epthianura aurifrons*

The Courage of Life

The Eastern Yellow Robin is found in south eastern and eastern Australia, mostly in coastal regions. It prefers dark shaded areas in woodlands or rainforests, and also ventures into parks and gardens in urban areas.

The robin's diet consists of insects, spiders and small invertebrates, and they use a 'perch and pounce' method of securing their prey.

These robins mate for life, and live out their lives within a small territory. They build their nests in the fork of a tree, often not more than five metres from the ground, and usually hatch two young.

Fledglings

A handful of sticks in a tree
A lining of hair;
A fledgling's hungry mouth,
And a wing on the air;
Here is the courage of life
Here of its heart the core,
Ask of the pride that is man
Has he more!

Mary Gilmore (1865–1962)

Eastern Yellow Robin, *Eopsaltria australis*

In the Dark of the Night

The Boobook is the smallest Australian owl and the female is larger than the male. It is one of five Australian members of the family of hawk-owls. We also have two barn owls, the sooty and the lesser sooty owls.

Owls have flat faces and forward-directed eyes, strong hearing, sharp beaks and flexible talons. They hunt at night and their prey includes small mammals such as possums and rodents.

Together with frogmouths, nightjars and the ground-dwelling bush stone-curlew, the owls make up Australia's nocturnal birds.

The 'mopoke' of the boobook owl is one of the best known of Australian bird-calls, and one that has caused much discussion for many years past. According to the fancy of the hearer the bird calls 'mopoke', or 'morepork', or 'boobook' or even 'cuckoo'. Ornithologists and aborigines favour 'boobook', most Australians favour 'mopoke', or 'morepork', while the first white inhabitants favoured 'cuckoo', the best-loved bird-call of their remote homeland. They were inclined to say that, in the land of their enforced residence, where every thing was upside down, where the sun shone in the north window instead of the south, where Christmas came at the wrong time of the year, and where trees dropped their bark instead of their leaves, the cuckoo (a day bird in Great Britain) was, of course, a night bird here.

From 'Australia's Owls', Dr. J. A. Leach, Argus, 6 January 1923

Boobook Owl, *Ninox novaeseelandiae*

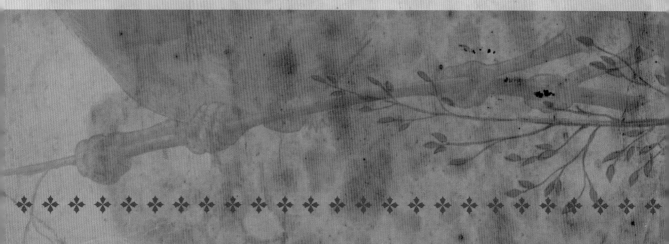

A Bird in the Hand...

The Gouldian Finch is one of Australia's most beautiful birds – which has proved a problem for these boldly coloured little grassfinches. They are truly distinctive. While all females and most males have black heads, around twenty-five per cent of males have red heads and some have gold heads. Why? We don't know.

Found in large numbers by white settlers in their natural habitat of the tropical north of Australia, the finches became a must-have item for every keen ornithologist and bird collector in the world. In those days the adage 'a bird in the hand is worth more than two in the bush' was taken very seriously indeed.

While large numbers are still bred in captivity, the Gouldian Finch in the wild has long been in decline, due to bird trapping, disease, fires and competition from livestock for the grasses it feeds on. In 1992 the species was declared endangered, and a conservation program is in place.

Gouldian Finch, *Erythrura gouldiae*

A Glimpse of Eternity

An apparently simple decision – such as going into the garden to better hear the exquisite song of a bird – can lead to a glimpse of eternity.

Graeme Gibson, *The Bedside Book of Birds*, 2005

A correspondent from Rushworth, Victoria, writes: 'A pretty little bird spent its New Year holidays in my garden…It somewhat resembled willie wagtail, but was brownish in colour, with some characteristics of "cranky fan" – the grey fantail. This little fellow's fantail of which it seemed to be as proud as a peacock was gorgeously coloured and in the sunlight it appeared to be bronze with a light halo around it. Its movements were extraordinarily quick and it darted like lightning through shrubs and under bushes after insects. I may be somewhat astray in my description as only for an instant did the little creature settle and relax.' There's no mistaking Mr. Robinson's bird as the gem-like rufous fantail – a sight to delight any bird observer. It has an attractive and peculiar song and moves about a great deal. Usually it is only seen in Victorian forest gullies during summer months.

From 'Nature Notes', David Fleay, Argus, 5 April 1941

Rufous Fantail, *Rhipidura rufifrons*

The Kick of the Cassowary

Beware the cornered Southern Cassowary! This flightless bird, which can grow to the height of 1.8 metres, is the world's most dangerous bird. It is the cassowary's feet that you should be wary of. They end in three strong sharp claws, the middle one up to seventeen centimetres long, which can disembowel a human intruder.

If left unchallenged, the cassowary is a shy creature whose silky black plumage allows it to blend into the undergrowth of its rainforest habitat in northern Queensland and New Guinea. They lead solitary lives, and survive on the fruit of the forest trees.

When it comes to breeding, the smaller male cassowary woos the dominant female, which lays the eggs in the male's territory before being driven off. The male then takes responsibility, incubating the eggs and feeding the young for up to nine months before they become independent.

The Southern Cassowary has been listed as endangered in Australia, and the due to the widespread clearance of rainforests in New Guinea the species is considered vulnerable worldwide.

Southern Cassowary, *Casuarius casuarius*

Survivors

The life expectancy of birds relates partly to their size. Bigger birds, seabirds and tropical birds tend to live longer than smaller ones. The albatross can live longer than most humans.

Birds in the wild tend to have short average life spans, since so many baby birds fail to survive their first weeks. But of those that do reach adulthood, a superb fairy wren, banded in the Australian Bird and Bat Banding scheme, survived for over ten years before being killed by a cat, a magpie is known to have survived twenty-three years, and the average lifespan of the short-tailed shearwater is thirteen years, with at least one reaching the grand old age of thirty-seven.

In contrast to their fellows in the wild, pet parrots tend to live very long lives with a select few of the larger parrots living more than one hundred years.

Perhaps the oldest bird in Australia was 'Cocky Bennett', whose obituary notice appeared in a Sydney paper in 1916. He was said to be 120 years old. In his later years 'Cocky Bennett' was practically featherless, and he used to scream out, 'One feather more and I'll fly'. This ancient bird was one of the common white, yellow-crested cockatoos which were first made known in 1790, two years after the first Australian settlement was established at Sydney.

From 'Notes for Boys', Alec H. Chisholm, Argus, 13 February 1936

Sulphur-crested Cockatoo, *Cacatua galerita*

The Sounds of the Australian Bush

A chorale of magpies carolling in the eucalypts at dawn is the sound of the Australian countryside. Wake to the cackle of kookaburras and you know you are in the Australian bush.

Australia's birds have unique and beautiful songs. Some, like the raucous shriek of the Sulphur-Crested Cockatoo, you can't avoid. Others, like the sweet trill of the playful wren, you will hear only if you stop and listen.

About an hour before sunrise, the woods are vocal with song…[August] is indeed the month of melody. Now may be heard the incessant cooing of pigeons, the peculiar note of the whipbird (Psophodes crepitans); the liquid song of the sacred kingfishers (Halcyon collaris); the mingled warbling of various Acanthiza [thornbills] and Malurus [wrens]; and the rejoicing notes of the robin redbreast…and the lately returned swallows. They who say our birds are songless should spend a little while in some dwelling near these thick tangled woods, and they would find that the error might have arisen from their having dwelt in towns or places where would-be sportsmen had destroyed most of the feathered tribes.

Sydney Morning Herald, 10 September 1860

Fairy Wren, *Malurus splendans*

Major Mitchell's Cockatoo

Major Mitchell's Cockatoo is a shy member of the generally bold and strident cockatoo family. It is found in the arid and semi-arid interior of all states and territories of Australia where it forages on the ground and amongst low foliage for native seeds, fruits, nuts and roots.

Also known as the pink cockatoo, it socialises with Galahs and Little Corellas, and lives in pairs or small flocks. Both male and female can spend years in a flock before mating.

In contrast to many of its relatives, this cockatoo has not adapted to land clearance and introduced plant species, and the reduction in its preferred woodlands habitat has lead to a decline in its numbers.

Major Mitchell's Cockatoo was discovered in 1831 and is named after the explorer and surveyor-general, Major Sir Thomas Mitchell.

Few birds more enliven the monotonous hues of the Australian forest than this beautiful species whose pink-coloured wings and flowing crest might have embellished the air of a more voluptuous region.

Major Sir Thomas Mitchell (1792–1855)

Major Mitchell's Cockatoo, *Cacatua leadbeateri*

Signalling the Dawn

Kookaburras play an important role in the culture of Indigenous Australians across the continent. Many Aboriginal legends draw a connection between the kookaburra's pre-dawn chorus and the break of day. In some, the kookaburra is commissioned by the spirits to call before dawn so that the other birds and animals can wake and enjoy the beauty of the sunrise. Other stories celebrate the kookaburras' snake-killing skills. Still others play on the Laughing Kookaburra's mocking laugh.

The Blue-winged Kookaburra has an equally distinctive call, which is more a guttural bark than a chuckle. Originally called the 'Barking Jackass' and the 'Howling Jackass', it is found in northern Australia in the coastal areas of Western Australia, the Northern Territory, Queensland and northern New South Wales.

Blue-winged Kookaburra, *Dacelo leachii*

Rose Robin

Australia has five red robins, which belong to the Petroica family. The Rose Robin, the smallest of them all, is found along the east coast of Australia from central Queensland to eastern South Australia. As with all our robins, the densely coloured breast is a sign of a mature male.

The Rose Robin breeds from September to January in the cool wet gullies and rainforests, then migrates to warmer, more open habitats in autumn and winter, when it is more likely to be seen. Though Australia's robins reminded the early British settlers of the European robins, they are not related.

Hope

'Hope' is the thing with feathers
That perches in the soul,
And sings the tune—without the words,
And never stops at all,
And sweetest in the gale is heard;
And sore must be the storm
That could abash the little bird
That kept so many warm.
I've heard it in the chillest land,
And on the strangest sea;
Yet, never, in extremity,
It asked a crumb of me.

Emily Dickinson, 1861

Rose Robin, *Petroica rosea*

Proverbial Birds

The early bird catches the worm

A bird in the hand is worth two in the bush

A rooster one day, a feather duster the next

As proud as a peacock

Birds of a feather flock together

Don't count your chickens before they hatch

To kill two birds with one stone

Lighter than a feather

Like a duck to water

Like water off a duck's back

One swallow does not a summer make

Something to crow about

Stone the crows

To be up with the lark

What is good for the goose is good for the gander

You can cage a bird, but you cannot make him sing

✦ ✦

Splendid Fairy-wren, *Malurus splendens*
Red-backed Fairy-wrens, *Malurus melanocephalus*

The Superb Fairy-wren

The Superb Fairy-wren, also known as the blue wren and jenny wren, is a delightful bird, much loved by those who know it. It inhabits the open native bushland of south-east Australia and also appears in urban backyards and gardens, usually in family groups of three or four.

When breeding, the female fairy-wren establishes a territory, which her partner and young sons help her defend. All daughters, once fully-fledged, are forced out of the home territory to find their own territory and partner. The female wren is responsible for building and repairing the nest.

An Australian National University study has discovered that the female's young are frequently not those of its partner. Instead they may be those of the local alpha male, a bird that moults earlier than other males and spends the months up to the breeding season preening and showing off his brilliant blue plumage to the females.

The Superb Fairy-wrens have distinctive long tails and long legs, and the breeding males boast the beautiful blue plumage, while the females, non-breeding males and young are a soft grey-brown.

Superb Fairy-wren, *Malurus cycneus*

Gang-gang Cockatoo

Cockatoos belong to the bird family Cacatuidae, which includes corellas, the cockatiel and the galah, as well as nine distinct species of cockatoo. One thing they have in common which distinguishes them from their close relatives, the parrots, is a movable crest.

Cockatoos are communal birds and they roost in flocks in the treetops at night. Like most parrots, they mate for life, and during the day they forage in family groups, with the young gathered together.

Gang-gang Cockatoos are found in south-east Australia, in the stringy bark forests of the Grampians, the Australian Alps, the Blue Mountains and the Snowy Mountains.

Like most cockatoos and many parrots, they like to nest in hollow logs and cavities in old trees. The Gang-gang are now vulnerable in some areas due to the clearance of old-growth forests. They remain conspicuous in Canberra's parks and garden areas in winter, where they feed off the introduced hawthorn bushes as well as their preferred eucalypts.

The Gang-Gang Cockatoo
Makes a terrible to-do,
Because he is an anarchist,
And bolshevistic, too.
He wears a bright red cap,
And he is a noisy chap,
For he loves to lead a riot,
And he loves a little scrap.
He dodges all bird-policeman
Because he doesn't want to hang;
And they, in turn, don't chase him,
When he's flying with his gang.

W.J., Sydney Morning Herald, 11 November 1933

Gang-gang Cockatoo, *Callocephalon fimbriatum*

The Trees are Felled

Most Australian parrots, cockatoos, lorikeets, owls, kookaburras and kingfishers nest in the hollows of dead or living trees, old standing wood and fallen trees. Up to seventeen per cent of birds in south-eastern Australia rely on these tree hollows and cavities for nesting and many return to the same nesting site each breeding season.

These old trees are around one hundred years old and the hollows and cavities have been caused by termites or fungi, by lightning, rain or wind, or by fire damage. When branches break off and fall to the forest floor, or rot suspended in the foliage, they provide excellent nesting sites. Eucalypts, particularly the red river gum, mountain gum, mountain grey gum and yellow box, all have hollows.

Eucalypts also tend to shed their lower branches, leaving an exposed area in which birds can create their own hollows.

One of the major threat to many of these native birds is the reduction in their habitat which leaves them without nesting sites. Old-growth forests cannot be easily replaced. Land clearance for agricultural purposes has left the Superb Parrot vulnerable in New South Wales and a number of parrots, including the Red-tailed Black Cockatoo and the Swift Parrot, are now endangered.

Woodlands are also being cleared and harvested for firewood, and the removal of dead wood and woody debris involved in fireproofing semi-rural properties also has its impact.

They came!…

They come no more. The cities have laid waste
The land where once the hosted wings flocked home.
The trees are felled – or ash Seed-time of grass
And blossoming of flower wake not again
As harvest of the wild. And we? Are we
More permanent than these that we displaced?
The wilderness returned; the dust of time
On Tyre and us alike keeps up; the thing
Man slays, slays him…To us the desert creeps.
And as it creeps, what debts, what debts it makes us pay!

From The Birds, Mary Gilmore, 1939

Pale-headed Rosella, *Platycercus adscitus*

Canary in the Coal Mine

Many species of Australian birds are facing uncertain futures. As the human population has spread out, habitat loss and degradation have had a major impact on bird populations. The recent Australian drought has caused extra stress and climate change will present ongoing difficulties.

The Action Plan for Australian Birds is a federal government initiative that has adopted the International Union for Conservation of Nature's definition of what constitutes a threat to a species.

According to the IUCN, a vulnerable species is one that faces a twenty per cent decline in population numbers over ten years, or three generations, whichever is longer. Australia has listed eighty three native birds as vulnerable.

An endangered species is one that faces a population reduction of fifty per cent over that same period of time. We have forty-one endangered species.

The critically endangered species are those that face an eighty per cent chance of become extinct within ten years or three generations, whichever is longer.

'Canary in the coal mine' – which comes from a time when miners knew that if their caged canaries toppled over it meant imminent asphyxiation for them – is not just an empty phrase: where birds are dying now (through poisons, habitat destruction and famine), people will die later. The die-off of seabirds, for instance, signals a die-off in sea life, including fish. It doesn't take a very smart augur to read that omen.

Margaret Atwood, *Guardian*, 9 January 2010

Variegated Fairy-wren, *Malurus lamberti*

A Magnificent Sight

The Galah, also known as the rose-breasted cockatoo or the pink and grey, is found across most of Australia. It is the most numerous of cockatoos and these days its population in settled areas is increasing.

Galahs quickly adapted to the changes in habitat brought about by white settlement, and, in turn, many were adopted as pets by the settlers. Early Australian newspapers abound with lost-and-found notices about Galahs who call 'coo-ee' or answer to the name of 'Jacky'. 'Galah' soon crept into the Australian vernacular to mean 'fool'.

Early last century Galahs were shot in large numbers. They are ground feeders and pose a threat to crops. They were also used in trap-shooting competitions in northern Victoria, despite complaints from bird preservation societies.

At first you meet him in little 'mobs' of 10 or 20 – for he is a gregarious bird – but as you proceed on your western course, he becomes more numerous, being at Hay and beyond met with in flocks of several thousands.

At all times the galah is extremely picturesque, but more especially when seen in these vast flocks…when you have drawn too near, there is a flush of rosy light, a rattle like miniature musketry from the flapping wings, and the immense body is in the air. They wheel in perfect unison like some well-drilled army – perhaps several times – and the effect of the alternate flashing of silver and pink, as their silver-grey backs and bright rosy breasts and underwings, respectively come into sight, is magnificent.

'The Galah', J.T.D., Sydney Morning Herald, 27 July 1907

Galah, *Eolophus roseicapillus*

Stop, Look and Listen

Birds offer us a delightful pastime. At its most basic, birding is cost free and rewarding.

How do you begin? You simply open your eyes and your ears and start noticing the birds that are all around you. You won't have to go far. The birds – and not just the pigeons, the sparrows, the maggies and the crows – are already there, it's just that you haven't taken the time to observe them.

Start with your own backyard or front door step. Most of us are moving way too fast to even hear that the birds are singing as we take a short cut through the local park. But if you listen, then stop, watch and wait until the bird reveals itself, you will begin to see what this birding is all about.

Soon you will want to identify the bird you see. Take note of its size, colouring, the shape of its body, its style of flight, and the sound it makes. Then find a field guide to Australian birds in your local library and see if you can spot it. If it is native, it will be there for sure.

If you have come this far, you are on the way. Birding is an enthusiasm shared by a many people from all walks of life and for some, once you start, there is no going back.

I hope you love birds too. It's economical. It saves going to heaven.

Emily Dickinson (1830–1886)

Rainbow Bee-eater, *Merops ornatus*

What Every
Birder Needs:

A pair of binoculars:	Consider what you can afford (a pair of poor binoculars is better than no binoculars at all) and if you plan to hike for some distance, consider the weight.
Clothing:	Choose clothes (they are probably already in your wardrobe) that are comfortable to walk, kneel and crouch in, and something that will blend in with the environment.
The capacity (and willingness) to remain still:	This is crucial.
Fellow enthusiasts:	Join a local birdwatching group and share your experiences.
A notepad and pencil:	Write a description of the bird you see to help you identify it later. Describing the bird will fine-tune your observation skills.
A field guide:	You will need this to identify the birds you see.
Camera:	A simple digital camera will be adequate.

Eastern Rosella, *Platycercus eximius*

A Twitcher's Dream

'Twitchers' take birdwatching to a new level. They check the birds they see off a list, and travel long distances to see rare birds. For some, twitching is a competitive pastime; others simply enjoy the thrill of observing as many birds as they can.

The Little Kingfisher, a quick shy bird that is Australia's smallest kingfisher, is a twitcher's dream.

At about twelve centimetres, it is the world's second smallest kingfisher. Its upper body is a brilliant blue and, like the Azure Kingfisher, it dives from low branches deep into the water to catch fish or small crustaceans. It may also hover over its prey.

The Little Kingfisher is found in the coastal regions of northern Queensland and the top end of the Northern Territory. It breeds from October to March and both parents use their long sharp beaks to burrow deep into creek banks or termite mounds to create a nest.

Little Kingfisher, *Ceyx pusillus*

Parrots in Literature

Alexander the Great is said to have returned to Greece from his conquest of the Persian Empire in 327 B.C. bearing a parrot from India.

About three hundred years later, the Roman poet Ovid wrote 'The Dead Parrot': 'Our parrot, winged mimic of the human voice, set from India's Orient, is dead.'

Parrots have been flitting in and out of literature ever since.

One of the first Australian children's books was *Who Killed Cockatoo?* which was written and illustrated by W.A. Cawthorne, and published in Adelaide in 1862.

Parrots also played a crucial role in Gustave Flaubert's *Un Coeur simple* (1877), *Wide Sargosso Sea* (1966), by Jean Rhys and, perhaps most memorably, *Treasure Island* (1883), by Robert Louis Stevenson.

Here's Cap'n Flint. I calls my parrot Cap'n Flint—after the famous buccaneer—here's Cap'n Flint predicting success to our v'yage. Wasn't you, Cap'n?'

And the parrott would say, with great rapidity, 'Pieces of eight! Pieces of eight! Pieces of eight!' till you wondered that it was not out of breath, or John threw his handkerchief over the cage.

'Now that bird,' he would say, 'is maybe two hundred years old, Hawkins—they live forever mostly; and if anybody's seen more wickedness, it must be the devil himself. She's sailed with England, the great Cap'n England, the pirate. She's been at Madagascar, and at Malabar, and Surinam, and Providence, and Portobello. She was at the fishing up of the wrecked plate ships. It's there she learned 'Pieces of eight', and little wonder; three hundred and fifty thousand of 'em, Hawkins! She was at the boarding of the viceroy of the Indies out of Goa, she was: and to look at her you'd think she was a babby. But you smelt power, didn't you Cap'n?'

'Stand by to go about,' the parrot would scream.

From Treasure Island, Robert Louis Stevenson, 1883

Eastern Rosella, *Platycercus eximius*

Purple-crowned Fairy-wrens

The Purple-crowned Fairy-wrens live in two distinct populations in the far north of Australia, which are divided by four hundred kilometres. One, *Malurus coronatus coronatus* can be found in the Kimberley region of Western Australia and the Northern Territory, and the other, *Malurus coronatus macgillivaryi*, inhabits the coastal regions from the Roper River in the Northern Territory to the Flinders River in Queensland.

The male wrens boast a black-and-purple crown during the breeding season, as well as the distinctive blue tail. The wrens nest in the thick vegetation that grows alongside the fresh-water creeks and rivers, and their numbers have diminished. They are now registered as vulnerable, due to the changes to their habitat caused by clearance, bushfires and the spread of weeds. A program is currently under way at the Mornington Wildlife Sanctuary in Western Australia to save the Purple-crowned Fairy-wrens.

Be like the bird, who
Pausing in his flight
On limb too slight,
Feels it give way beneath him
Yet sings
Knowing he has wings.

Victor Hugo (1802–1885)

Purple-crowned Fairy-wren, *Malurus coronatus*

The Joy of Exultant Things

Australian Magpies are found across the nation in all but the northern most tips of Queensland and the Northern Territory and the driest desert areas of Western Australia.

They mix happily with humans in urban areas and often a family group adopts a home and backyard as its territory, scaring other birds away and sharing the yard with family pets. The female builds a nest of sticks, high in a tree, and the male and last year's young help raise the nestlings.

Magpies come in different shapes and sizes in different parts of the country. There are now eight subspecies of the one species recognised. The largest is the most common: the Black-backed Magpie is found on the east coast of Australia from Melbourne to Brisbane. The Tasmanian Magpie with its very short beak, and the Northern Territory Magpie, which has a long slender bill, are the two smallest magpies.

We humans tend to have a love/hate relationship with magpies, prompted only in part by the football teams named after them. During the four-to-six week nesting season, the occasional male magpie becomes very aggressive and swoops all who stray into its territory. Using an umbrella will protect you; waving sticks above your head helps; cyclists can try drawing eyes on the back of their helmets. If possible, avoid the area until the season passes.

Magpies

I hear the cry of the magpies joyously gushing
Over the morning,
The carolling slogan of magpies, like a rill rushing,
And sorrow scorning.

Magpies, fill up my heart with the joy of exultant things
Fresh notes adorning!
Breath of the morning primeval your melody brings
To thrill my morning.

Louis Esson (1878–1943)

Australian Magpie, *Gymnorhina tibicen*

All Lovely Things

The Chestnut Teal is a beautiful little dabbling duck that lives in the coastal swamps and wetlands of Australia's south-east and south-west. It can be found in saline, brackish or fresh water.

Ducks tend to be either 'divers', which duck deep into the water to find their food, or 'dabblers' which have smaller feet and skim the water surface and dip into the shallows to feed.

The male Chestnut Teal has the beautiful green head, while the female is easily mistaken for the Grey Teal, which has a distinguishing white throat.

While New South Wales, Queensland, Western Australia and the Australian Capital Territory have outlawed recreational duck shooting, it is still permitted in South Australia, Tasmania, Victoria and the Northern Territory.

South Australia and Victoria also have open seasons on the native Stubble Quail. The duck and quail are shot with shotguns, which rarely kill the birds outright, and many are left to suffer and die.

As the art of life is learned, it will be found at last that all lovely things are necessary:– the wild flowers by the wayside, as well as the tended corn; and the wild birds and creatures…

From 'Unto This Last', John Ruskin, 1860

Chestnut Teal, *Anas castanea*

Northern Rosella

Australia's recent drought brought some of our most colourful rosellas into urban areas for the first time. The birds make lively visitors. Rosellas are divided into two main groups: those with blue cheeks, which include the Crimson Rosella, and the white-cheeked Eastern Rosella, Northern Rosella and Pale-headed Rosella. The Western Rosella, which is found only in the south-west of Western Australia, has distinct yellow cheek patches. The rarest of the rosellas is the Northern Rosella, which is found in the savannah country of the top end of Australia, from the Kimberleys through to the Gulf of Carpentaria.

At noon in the forest

Morning and evening, the Australian forest is awake; at noon it is asleep. No greater contrast can be imagined than between the morning hours and those at mid-day. In the former, the very flowers seem to possess an active existence. Myriads of such, larger and more brilliant than those under English skies, load the air with the sweetest scents; magnificent tree-ferns wave their fronds or branches in the light breeze; on old stumps of trees great green and yellow lizards lie watching for their prey; the magpie throws her voice from the wattles, and possibly the lyre-bird in the denser scrub; and in the tall gums numberless parrakeets, parrots, rosellas, cockatoos, butcher-birds, lover-birds, &c., are screaming and darting to and fro. But by-and-by the intense heat will silence all these, and nothing will be heard but the chirp of the grasshopper and the shrill sound of some unseen insect. At twilight again there is a revival of life, but not of so cheerful a description. The cicadas shriek by myriads their deafening 'p-r-r-r-r-r'; drowsy opossums snarl in the gum-boles, and flocks of cockatoos scream as some great gray kangaroo bounds past them like a belated ghost. If there is marshy ground near, the deep boom of the bittern, the wail of the curlew, and the harsh cry of the crane, mingling possibly with those of a returning or passing flock of black swans, will add to the concert. In a moment of silence one may be startled by the mocking laughter of the jackass, or the melancholy 'mo-poke' (or 'more-pork') of the bird of that name. The dead of night is not so still as the universal hush of the burning noon.

From 'Chambers's Journal', reprinted in New York Times, 18 January 1880

Northern Rosella, *Platycercus venstus*

Bird Vigilance

Feral cats in the wild and domestic cats in urban areas pose a threat to birds. Domestic cats should be neutered and wear a bell on their collar. Ideally cats should be kept inside or in enclosed runs. If your cat runs free, keep it inside at dawn and dusk, the times when the birds are most vulnerable.

Window strike: If a bird flies into your window, it will most likely to be stunned, so keep it safe from predators until it recovers consciousness.

Insecticides can poison birds as well as killing off the insects (not just the ones you want to kill) that birds feed on.

Many birds are hit by cars when they fly into their path on the roads.

Foxes are a danger to small ground feeding birds in the wild and in some urban environments too.

Predators such as eagles, hawks and owls also threaten the lives of native birds. The native Crested Pigeon has been found to emit a warning whistle on take-off through its flapping wings, which alerts fellow pigeons to danger.

How constantly alert birds are, whether flying, feeding, or courting, and even in their very songs. I was listening absently to the rich notes of a rufous whistler just outside, when the spirited song stopped so abruptly in mid-phrase that I stepped onto the veranda to see. There was no prowling cat about, but I noticed that all twittering and chirruping in the garden had ceased. Then I saw a bird of prey, sailing about far up in the blue. It is not easy to take a bird unawares.

'The Bushlover's Notes' Fabian, Courier Mail, 21 April 1934

Budgerigar, *Melopsittacus undulatus*

Bibliography

Australian Bush Birds in Colour, Irene & Michael Morcombe, Reed, 1974

Birds Australia: www.birdsaustralia.com.au

Australian Museum & Birds Australia: birdsinbackyards.net

Birdlife International: www.birdlife.org

Birds in Literature, Leonard Lutwak, University Press of Florida, 1994

Collected Verse of Mary Gilmour, Volume 2, edited by Jennifer Strauss, The Academy Editions of Australian Literature

Gould League: www.gould.edu.au

How and When the Lyrebird was Discovered, A.H. Chisholm, State Library of Victoria

John Shaw Nielson, edited by Cliff Hanna, University of Queensland Press, 1991

100 Birds to See Before You Die, David Chandler & Dominic Couzens, The Five Mile Press, 2008

Parrots of Australia Green Guide, Terence Lindsey, New Holland, 1998

Private Lives: Ages, Mates and Movements of Some Australian Birds, Pauline Reilly, Kangaroo Press, 1988

The Bedside Book of Birds, Graeme Gibson, Bloomsbury, 2005

The Birdwatcher's Notebook, Peter Slater, Weldon, 1988

The Endeavour Journal of Sir Joseph Banks, 1768–1771, Vol 11, edited by J.C. Beaglehole, Angus & Robertson, 1962

The Field Guide to the Birds of Australia, Graham Pizzey & Frank Knight, Harper Collins, 2007 (8th edition)

About the Illustrator & Author

Illustrator Shirley Barber

Australian author/artist Shirley Barber grew up
on the isle of Guernsey, surrounded by fern filled
water lanes, wildflower fields and hedgerows.
When she came to live in Australia over forty-five
years ago, Shirley was amazed by the strange and
brilliantly coloured native birds. Though best
known to millions of children for the fairytales
she has written and illustrated, Shirley has a wide
collection of native bird paintings which have
been published in calendar form for sixteen years.

Author Margaret Geddes

Margaret Geddes is a Melbourne writer who grew up in country Victoria. Her previous
publications include *The Australian Garden, Blood, Sweat & Tears, Remembering Weary* and a novel,
Unseemly Longing.